SALVAGED
MAXIMS

D1057629

SALVAGED

MAXIMS

Poems by Naton Leslie

Word Press

Published by Word Press
P.O. Box 541106
Cincinnati, OH 45254-1106

Editor: Kevin Walzer
Business Editor: Lori Jareo

Visit us on the Web at www.word-press.com

ISBN: 0-9708667-9-8
LCCN: 2002104793

Typeset in Industrial by WordTech Communications,
Cincinnati, OH

Author photo: Lynn Rogers

Cover artwork: "Iris," monotype by Mary Kathryn Jablonski

ACKNOWLEDGMENTS

The following poems have appeared in the magazines listed here, sometimes in slightly different forms: "Last Word" and "Speaking in Relics" in *Arkansas Review*; "The Growing Anger of Men" in *Poem*; "If He's Faking It, He Has a Lesson to Teach the Other Birds," and "The Last Go-Round" in *Interim*; "Sedative: What I Have Learned to Do," in *The Dickinson Review*; "Cell Division" and "Blue Laws," in *American Literary Review*; "Lost and Found" in *Riverwind*; "The Whole Law" and "The Margins of Mirage" in *The Chariton Review*; "Hadji" in *Sulpher River Literary Review*; "For Amelia Earhart" in a Red Hen Press anthology, and "Speaking in Relics" and "Lost and Found," reprinted in *The Second Word Thursdays Anthology* (Bright Hill Press).

Grateful acknowledgment is made to the National Endowment for the Arts for fellowship support which made the completion of this book possible. Finally, many thanks to Jonathan Blumberg who reprinted "The Growing Anger of Men" in *Unbottled* and who patiently read each section of this book as it twisted and crept into being.

The quoted passages which serve as epigrams to these poems can be found in *The Grounds and Maxims of the English Laws* by William Noy (6th Edition, Dublin: 1792). The book was once owned by John McCleare, signature dated 1882. It then passed into the hands of Dabney J. Carr, who crossed out McCleare's name and added his own, without date. I purchased the leather bound volume in a junkshop in 1984.

Of Political And Moral Rules

Of Tenures, Deeds & Heir

INTRODUCTION

LOST AND FOUND

*Introduction to the Matters contained
in the following Treatise.*

In slouching quarters, slipped
into towns which accept them
like hesitant apologies, junk-
shops are bad boys of commerce,
the weird cousin, the hermit

of stores, parking lot filled
with goods like a mob has formed,
hoarding the once prized
flotsam of our lives
only the landfill should know,
the reminders of our fickle
love of the plug-ugly and
the world's transformed things.

What we put on the curb crawls
away to them, defeated or even
maimed. We have not thrown them
away—we have chased them, harried
the baby carriage with wheels
askew, the box of books
from uncle's attic, the outmoded
mower, the toys we keep all
of our joyous lives.

In the junkshop they find
salvation, and a limbo
of heaps and shelves,

forming the eyesores our pasts
become, gathering the curious
and waiting on prayers.

THE WHOLE LAW

A Summary of the whole Law
divided into the Laws
of Reason, Custom and Statutes

1. *Reason*

You can always count on old Aristotle
to set you straight, get you on the dime.
It does not follow one can say,
and the law becomes a smug friend
who says I told you so. You cannot

join the bandwagon and play its tune,
pull Houdini's string of needles
from your mouth without defying
time, place and the body—I see you
smile. Yes, it pleases us to believe

the spilled salt made our car fail,
but it is the timing belt, not luck.
Testimonials are drivel, *ad hominem*
not the Leakeys' passion and
our belief in the crucial-fiction

or the moment of (re)insurrection lends
us a certitude which Aristotle, old
man of us all, would firmly declare
does not add up. Count it off:
Orderly, sensical, orderly, and *fair.*

2. *Custom*

Take off your hat.

We have the face cringing
at a mistaken fork, the misplaced
napkin, the missive sent to the dying
saying *Get Well Soon*, the ruined note
in the chorus when our voice is too loud,
the ms manners warning us not to invite
the naked friend under the mistletoe,
the misspoken sentiment when what we
meant was the missing beat of our heart.

Speak well of the dead.

When death makes us the missing,
we can only hope for glad reminiscence,
that asked to pray they will mist over
with the primed. Do not be fooled
by the mourning, they must be lulled
into drama when grief is in front
of God and everyone.

3. *The Statutes*

They are constants. You can always count on
them being there—unless someone hammers

them. Can you bear *The Pieta* with
its missing nose, the ancient bronzes

14

thrown overboard when salvage ships
foundered in two thousand-year-old storms?

These are the mysteries. Statues are
absolutes, like the gravity keeping

them poised like lives arrested when
most meaningful. Shouldn't we all

strive to freeze at that one moment
when we are found at the bottom,

at our best, torso muscles rippling
with the sea, our hands slaying Medusa,

propping up the fallen comrade or
even cradling God in our arms?

THE DICKER

*Also of bargaining
selling, restoring &c*

It's waiting at the junkshop:
the ellipse of the piano stool
you think can be righted,
a brass pole lamp you could
rewire and polish and save
from the scraper, from the next
shoulder at refuse's wheel,
so you go

to the man who does not care
if he ever sells what he has
not purchased, and you make
your impossible offer.

He looks at you as though
you have misspoken, a stare
which speaks of broken promises
and curses, as though the price
was a plague wished upon his
shop, that you have said
the unspeakable in his holy
presence. Yes, it would have
been better, the mouth nearly
says, the eyes do say, if you
had not put breath to such a lie,
a vileness, a falsehood, a slander,

a defiling price for so good
a good thing. Next he looks

away, shakes his head or
dismisses you with a wave
aimed to make you small
or disappear,

and then with a pause that says
I will play, he gives a figure.

Drop the item as though it burns.
Put your hands on your hips
and circle it. Find a flaw,
apologize for bringing it up
but do, do. Act as unsure
as first frost and then

give in a little more,
higher, but not the ceiling,
not ever. If it ends there

you must endure his litany
about dishonor and theft.
You don't know what you're getting
he'll say, and you are to feel
unworthy of the old oak bookcase
with the now-exposed cracked glass,
the split shelf, though the grain
is still as glorious as tides.

Or it begins again, the haggle
cotillion, the insinuations,
arms folded isometric, until

you are home with the thing itself,
faced by the fixing and sanding,

17

and like Hawthorne's witch who made
a broom a gentleman, you must bring
it back, give it the jig of life.

SEDATIVE: WHAT I HAVE
LEARNED TO DO

And as Controversie do often arise
I have set down how They may be
quietly ended

Sail away, give and get
fullness from fury. I stop
a man who is so drunk
the world is a hard road
through a brackish landscape,
and faces are twitching
billboards of disdain.

Half of his words are encoded,
the other half are obscene.

I send myself a telegram:
Fool loose on the planet Stop
Send vocabulary stop
but at this moment you are
teetering on Occam's Razor.
If you speak it is not sound,
walk and you've caused motion,
laugh and you bring rain,

and if you fight you have been
sliced by the illogical.

So be late summer still.
Watch his deltoids as they give
away his next step. Stone

your face, be as mute
as mystery, become elemental.
He needs explosions, but
when there is nothing
but you, even that will cease

to exist, and then some other
synapse might fire, if you are
lucky, and you are, and he
turns away a bit or a friend
comes up, saves his face
with a bit of bargaining.

Let it go, he murmurs,
what a friend says to the dying.
We're out of here.

The Margins of Mirage

The Rules of Reason are of two
Sorts. Some take from Learning,
as well as divine as human, and
some proper to Itself only.

Skepticism has been called
intellectual chastity—that said,
then belief must be a promiscuity,
giving it up for faith.

So do we owe submission when
the saint's hand does not decay
in the bell-jar? Are we to kiss
the clutch of knuckles or

be chaste and doubt the hoary claw?
I have only questions. Answers
whisper. Whom did Jacob wrestle?
How did he, one night until dawn

in the place he named *Penuel,*
strive with a god and prevail?

   * * *

In Findlay, Ohio, a man declared
the image of Jesus has appeared
in the growing rust
on a Marathon oil tank
at the end of a long dirt road.

They came to see the apparition.
Some claimed the figure of a child
was forming too, at the side
of the Lord, slowly etched
in the divine oxide. They came
in greater numbers, layering
the country lane with clay plumes
in the pressured heat of July.

At the local gas station they sold
the image of Jesus of the Oil Tank
on tee-shirts and coffee mugs,
I Saw Jesus in Findlay, Ohio
bumper stickers and buttons.
They sprayed the road with tar.

Choked by roiling dust,
the fine yellow clay
filtering under doors, sills,
down drains from clothes, hair,
a chaste figure approached
at night and covered
the hallowed image with
a purge of red paint. Later,
he was arrested, undone
and in some unspoken state,
huddled in the sanctified weeds
of his nearby, unplowed field.

OF THEOLOGY
& GRAMMAR

Last Word

The Acts of Parliament
which refrain ecclesiastical
Persons from committing Waste
in their Possessions

Gold
shark skin suits and
bright lights and
wouldn't you know,
the whole choir behind them,
beatific, rhythmic,
and well-paid. These are

the divine messengers
of our common era.
They mouth the multiple,
pearly and pear-shaped
syllables, tears
on their oily faces,
like a full moon in
the juicy sky—aren't they
handsome, dressed to-the-nines,
pretty as an Easter child?

I am chaste and poorly clad.
A young woman who thought
she could love me
gave me a pair of Jimmy Swaggart
cufflinks after his bleary,
carnal confession. They bore

a picture of the coiffured one
hovering a hand over the head
of a child. Good man, Jimmy.

Let's get this straight.
This is about laws and rights
and the underpinnings of what
can no longer be named
civilization. We have played
out the divine kite in a storm
wind. God, you are loose
and on your own. Though you
have called it *forsaken*.

BLUE LAWS

Sunday is no Day in Law

Some days when I rise it is all
the list writhing in its fullness,

to do, to do its haunting moan.
On Sunday, cows stood stoic and

spilled their udders, the steam
engines thirsted in the hollow

factories, and the laundry hung
like the guilty. We are no longer

gripped by those days, the known
halting, only the orb turning,

or as we imagined, face bowed
to the sun god on this day

of the sun, motion arrested like
a stalled movie, the celluloid

framing the moment Bogart unwraps
the black falcon and Peter Lorrè

murmurs and sighs. Then the center
burns in the projector light.

I do not rest. I do not want to
stop. I do not want to spend

a seventh of my here-and-there life,
in hot collars, in the brave lap

of wooden benches, mumbling in
the stench of bibles, and later

my body invisibly thrashing in coiled
repose on doilied drawing room chairs.

IF HE'S FAKING IT, HE HAS
A LESSON TO TEACH THE OTHER BIRDS

Persons using Bull-Baiting or
Bear-Baiting, or such like
Sports on a Sunday, shall forfeit.

My father taught me to kill.
I remember first seeing a toad,
as a toddler, and in a tumbling
curiosity I tossed a pebble
to see it hop. My father called
from his lawn chair: *Stone him,*
boy, stone him! Aglow
in his laughter I destroyed
the creature with rocks.
For days I carried the body
with me. Years later,

he told me that woodpeckers,
those giant, gentlemen birds,
were blasting his trees
with their hammering probes.
So I've been shooting
the shit out of them.
I blanched, told him they were
not eating wood, only
the insects infesting the oaks
and ash he was defending.

All I know is that they peck
hell out of the trees.
So I kill them.

I just kill
anything like that,
anything what gets
close to the house.

The man is not brutish,
but I do not know how
to explain when he slays
chipmunks with a twelve gauge.
He has always tried to kill
the crows laughing
in the field—I have heard crows
are bored in their limited bodies.
He has mostly failed, but
tells me he has named
one crow "Hoppy," as it appears
to have only one leg.

I'd never shoot him, he says,
He's had it too hard.

Speaking in Relics

Of Grammar, the Rules are
Infinite in the Etymology
of a Word

My mother finds phrases
In her voice which surprise
Her like an overseas postcard
Fallen out of an old book.

There were boo-coo
People at the fair,

She will say, not realizing
Her mother, herself raised by
Grandparents, themselves not
Far fallen from settlers in

The heartless hard coal ridges
Of Pennsylvania, those who were

Driven from Labrador by war,
Had saved *Beaucoup* for her
Like a secret recipe. And I
Embrace our own half

Junkshop language, lost and
Defeated by Celts, Romans,
Saxons and Normans, born German,
Made Latin and then left

For the whole world
To lilt and lift in

Perpetual *You know?* and *Okay?*
There is conquest and conjunction
In my breath, history in
My utterance, and I must remember

To remember the texts of those
Behind me, to be the one ahead.

BY YOURSELF

Spinster being an indifferent
Addition for Man or Woman.

This is the worst thing
you can say to a man or woman
living alone, either from
age, will, or the random
shots of accident and love:

You should not be
doing that by yourself.

Who will help them
trail garbage to the curb,
with bursitis and locked knees,
lift the fallen limb
under the fog and breathless
knock of a feathering heart?
But it is harder still

to endure the year's
flare of azalea in silence,
to laugh out loud
at the joke only you hear,
to think of the joke yourself,
the visit of your voice
suddenly saying something,

anything. Indifference
is not a matter of law,
it is what sits itself

across the table and makes
us wonder if the world

would stop if we had eggs
for dinner, last night's
pork and beans for breakfast,
if no one would notice
when we do not retrieve
the gladioli from the patch
we doggedly turned over,
a spade awkward in veined hands,
clearly what we should do alone.

OF LOGICK

A Barometric Body

*When the Cause ceaseth
the Effect also ceaseth.*

A bone cracked deep in the body,
a trunk-piece, a part not a limb,
leaves behind its own dialect,
its own species of posture and memory.

Spring revisits the cause
as shoulder muscles flex
in the fecund air,
in higher pressures of clear
skies or in the rains
making the earth pliant.

                Then a stiff
coil pops in the collar,
the hunch starts to the side,
the tools drop from the hand.
I revisit the fall which changed
the lithe to brittle,
the slip on ice and the moment
when the animal knows it has been
delivered a short time here.

Winter restages the scenario
as it slickens the way,
shrinks the tendons
like the barometer band,
the drying of leather,
and bindings which heal,

the bandages which embrace
the badly broken.

Too incantatory. Remember
your buddy Aristotle and
apply logic. Try again.

* * *

A cracked bone, deep in the body,
a trunk-piece, a part not a limb,
leaves behind its own prosody,
its custom of posture and mime.

Spring revisits the cause
in the warming, greening air,
as bridged shoulder muscles flex
in lifts of higher pressure.

The clarity of rains makes
the earth pliant. Then a stiff
coils snaps in the neck,
the collar hunches to the left,

the tools drop from the grasp.
I revisit the slip which changed
the lithe to brittle, the lapse
of step on ice, the flail and hang

of the moment when the animal
knows it has been delivered
a short time here—then the fall,
and the calm surety of the injured.

38

It's a wrap. Put it in the can.
Pay off the musicians. Let's
get out of here.

THE GROWING ANGER OF MEN

To make a Man swear to
bring me Money upon Pain
of Killing, and he
bringeth it accordingly
is Felony.

I have not told this before.
On the first day of school,
a day few recall but one marked
by our lamentations, I was
caught in the muscling of crowds,
the odor of lines, the feral
regimen of dedicated hours,
a grief for a lost home
flapping up like a bird let
loose in a room, when a boy
whose name I never knew
jumped on me outside. We fell
onto the hardpacked ground
and it was the first violence
I learned could be levied
by another child, the painful
exclamations of his small fists,
made worse by my surprise.
Then another boy pulled him off,
and thoroughly thrashed him,
then shook my hand and gave me
a name to remember later when
I met a man, Charlie Fisch, and
thanked him though he had forgotten.

I have never met an angel.
I have never met a man
who would take up a good
fight since. Later, when
even worse plagued me
I would take to the woods,
maple switch in hand
and behead jeering crowds
of wild carrot, or chase
milkweed from its smug pods
—or when older, stronger,
take wedges and sledge
and make a stack of firewood
from a winter fallen tree.

Once I fought a young man
goaded on by a weight of others,
and when we were spent, we stood,
shook hands, our puffy brows
roofing grins, though I had

threatened to chew off his ear
and spit it in his face when
he had me down. I didn't
mean it, it was posture
and he knew it. The next day
we laughed at our matching eyes.

There is a hard angel falling
now and its weight is like
a pallet of stones. I'm looking
for you, Charlie Fisch,
you who grew so odd and humble,
to turn up when the bully

is too much at my door,
standing in my way. But now
I am easing out from under
the knuckled weight, on my own,
making a devastation of the weeds,
a mad pile of wood behind the house.

ON THE SPOT

So where two Persons fight after a
former Quarrel, it shall be presumed
to be out of Malice.

This is a complicated story,
not a narrative but an unwinding
to a core. My father bore
a grudge like natural markings,
part of his skin, and a word

or ill-timed glance revealed
his enemies. When his father
gave out at breakfast, his wife

called for help and a neighbor
came, a man with whom my father
had drank and laughed for whole-

hearted evenings at the Blue Goose,
where they escaped the haints only
those born of those mountains can

see or name. Dee Gabler worked
when he could, on strip mines,
in a glass factory, and was known
to tickle clear hootch from
improbable sources—it could
make raccoons come down and claim
to be your close kin, allow
the clumsy to dance or fight,
and flip the real into cartoons.
But it was Dee

who held the dying man
until the spinning lights
diced the mountain sides, held him
as he spit up and was silenced
by too much work too often too fast.

* * *

One more layer and we have
Dee as conjureman, Stackalee,
as cougar conqueror able
to mutate into mountain fog.
He had gripped the full end.

My father felt denied the last
clasp of the old man's hand and
figured Dee either owed him that

or was otherwise to blame,
I could never tell which.
A month later I saw my father
and mother grapple over keys
in the damp dusk, and later
I was bundled into another car
and driven in the middle
of an acid March night
to the Clarion River bridge,

where my father, riotous
on Dee's wild liquor, was walking
the top of the metal span,
toe-over-toe, and when coaxed
down in the thrashing spotlights,
into the now spotty rain,

he kicked out the ribs of two men,
and bit through the hand of a third.
Dee then stepped out of the fog
and took him down with one blow.

This is the layer which remains,
which stands for an end. My father
has hated Dee ever since, for having
been at both of their deaths,
for the wound, a sucker punch
he called it. But I believe Dee
had stood between both men
and their fates, was guilty of
saving one and losing the other.

LANDMARKS AND SOUVENIRS

*The derived Power cannot be
greater than the primitive one.*

Pacific aboriginal thought
made singing a map, intoned
dreamscape lasting as long
as song itself, features
prefigured in narrative,
singing ancestor hills.
But this

is all second-hand, my
throat does not create
in quite that way. Let me
think with my eyes:

> mountain laurel crowds stones,
> large as lost Toltec heads,
> which have sledded down
> a Pennsylvania hillside,
> and water has made ice dollops
> around the creek fringe
> —pluck one from a stem
> and it disappears. At this

instant I am seven years old
and want to keep everything:
the deep hue of wet pebbles,
salamanders, twisted wood,
metal-green beetles,
my grandfather's rubber change

purse, a penny from his birth
and death years inside.
Oh how I wanted to keep.

Might I have snagged it all
with a song of coins and ice?
The world is storied,
but still we crush through it,
rudely gathering, pursuing
art, great ideas and loves

> while ice thaws on the cursed
> and arthritic dogwood, now
> blooming, the creek groans
> more deeply as it loosens,
> even the earthworms
> transcribe some landscape,
> silently making our loam.

ENTROPY

That which is not originally of Force
will not avail by length of Time.

I suspect order is largely
a lie. Quebec wants out
of an imperfect union,
bindings affixed by war
now bulge like overpacked
luggage. Now even furniture

retrieved from the itchy
skirmish for new is splitting
again, mortise, dovetail, half-
lap, rabbet, and blind dowel
complaining then wholly giving
way to dry heat and our dull

weight. The junkshop feeds
on our unlasting work. Every-
thing we fashion by force
or love is primed to bloom
as junk. Even I should have
been the son who could bear

great weights, fight well
and kill cleanly. But I dominate
only my own reflection, my father's
thumping chest overshadowing
in my willowy frame, allied
by alien genes, some suspected

of being French. Quebec wants
out and so do I. Still he tried
to teach me to box until a nerve
in my jaw proved it glass under
a sparring tap. I buckled and
dropped amid stars. Whoever

first wrote about eggs and kings
got it right
                —we are all fooling
ourselves in believing it can be
fixed, that we can preserve
the china from a secession
to pieces, roofs from infiltration

of water, hold a hanged man up
by the knees and say *breathe*,
or find our next son in orphan

new-to-you racks, one with all
the unities, a finely cut gib,
the perfect, reconstituted man.

UNDERPINNINGS

*A weak Foundation destroys
the Superstructure.*

We walked the old lane
to the family house, fallen
on its face like a movie set,
the front intact with its
hollow Potemkin windows,
the barn with its whole
tree beams rotted, a memory.

A memory: great-uncle Guy
came home from Bradford,
now a street car conductor.
He bought new straw hats
for the younger children,
a bit of the city to sit
upon their towheads. But
the neighbor boys flipped
them into the beaver pond.

Guy told them: *Get those hats*,
and when they didn't, waggling
their faces, he took them
by collar and waistband
and tossed them in
—they'd emerge, wary
as amphibians and then
they'd return like birds,
until one surfaced with
a handful of ruined straw.

I find those straws
in my hand now.
At the junkshop I am propelled
through mounds of scorched irons
and an orgy of blasted cane
bottom chairs, all memories,
ruined but saved.

They sit like fossil beginnings
and foundations, like neolithic
stone circles, some facade for
living or dying—now simply
signalling *I have been here* and
everyone might as well know it,
by plowing, mowing, stepping around
my boulders, my work, my discarded
religion, appliances, homesteads,
memories and hats.

ANTECEDENT GHAZAL

*A personal Action
dies with the Person.*

I cannot blame this ash which falls upon my head
on fires I did not start, the heat distant, thin.

Nor can I find fault with common laws or condemn
old houses we repair or tear apart with machines.

I will not invest guilt on Archimedes nor on old
mapmakers for those latitudes of devoured horses,

and you'll not catch me complaining about a beam
sagging now because long done carpenters did not

take me into calculation a full century and more
later, could not conceive these winters I endure.

I forget to cast aspersion on old lovers or upon
those warping maxim into guilt, tradition as sin.

We have a body of sin preserved by all those who
claim justice is not part truth—but let us ring

the bell for winter's end. In the past, workers
picked the best woods: wormy chestnut and slick

elm we stroke on junkshop tables and tool chests
or in the beams of barns we now slowly dismantle,

horse stalls better made than all our new houses,
massive bodies still present in the rubbed plank.

The old directions we still heed no longer apply
and will lead us astray, into breathless deserts

where their machines puff and burn the sky's far
layer, fires we cannot snuff, warmth we will rue.

HADJI

If a Man commit a Trespass in a Forest,
and dies, by Forest Law no Action will
lie for the Trespass.

1.

They were traced more than
a century ago, these root-rubbed
trails up Mount Marcy or others
called *Whiteface*, *Wolf-jaw*,
or *Giant*. I suppose old guides
bushwhacked them, the best routes
to bald, glacier-grooved cliffs
above the tree-lines, long views
after the climb's grunt and blow.

Once blazed they were sanctified
and named by the new state
lords of the Adirondacks,
the hoary guides long gone
and with them the way to other
faces unscaled, unmarked,
palimpsests of other vistas.

2.

At the trailhead, the genesis
of place, we scramble like
survivors along an engraved path
until we meet thinner air

at the top, the Ausable River
chasm at our feet, a dashing,
fatal possibility. Then
we are strangely arisen.
We do it again and again.

But every year some wander
beyond these scribed crossings,
outside the trails and then
into untrammeled stone, fallen
husks of birch, adolescent pine,

and are never found again.
they are few but holy, ones
who have read bramble's I-Ching
tried furtive springs, and deny
directions and despair, who light
fires hoping that someone misses
them, and will trace the slip
of smoke to their faces, lost vistas.

3.

They are trying to get down.
Where is the flat earth?
they ask, though they are
fully free, five days gone
and a front page story,
then twelve days away
and they are as incorruptible
as saints, even if found now
they are only a bundle
of nylon and nothing but
clutching and stillness,
blanched and sweetly broken,

beyond the *quid pro quo*
of prayer, in an unsullied
wilderness, only yards
from somewhere, so near us,
by a road through blueberry
wreathed stone and the temple
pillars of lodge pole pine.

Ruin and Replacement

A Greater contains a Less.

Marcus Aurelius begat Commodius
and blessed empire with entropy.
What follows must always be
diminished from a golden age.
Even home cannot be trusted
to remain unchanged, despite
our longings and foolish
heirs. I can still go home,

the town I now give that name,
first place, original packaging:
Youngstown, Ohio. It no longer
offers much, and all of us
who visit from farther places
call it *going back*, a reversal
or retreat, though we find
it is not there. Only a shell
remains, a fossil Youngstown,
a city remnant, an outline
of steel mills and factories
divided by gangster empires.

Maybe all ruins were made
by those who hated fully,
Persepolis leveled in revenge
by that mobster Alexander,
Mayan cities looted by other
gangs, the fragile jungle
another ruin. So when I hear
the blues, I hear endings:

Let's play those Toltec blues.
Let's hear that good old
Etruscan stomp, a Babylonian
boogie-woogie, the jazz
of Egyptians finding the Ka
is not forever, the old-time
Greek slave spirituals sung
in the Pompeii olive groves.

Abandon the cities, we keep
saying, and begin new places,
leave our relics behind:

Here's a wondrously preserved
fragment of Sears and Roebuck
cloth. The design tells us
it was used to protect
children from burning
in their beds—possibly
woven with asbestos.

Lead pipes made the Romans
insane and drought drove
the desert Anasazi from
their shard-rubbled hives.
When I look at mountains
I see old seas, plains
of massive animals grazing,
pushed to geologic heights

or twisting stone arches,
mesas, badland arabesques
or a waltz of gentled

uplifts in the Appalachians.
After enough time we become
our own unrecognizable spawn.

CAUGHT DEAD

An Adulterer takes the Wife
of another Man and new cloathes
Her, the Husband may take with
his Wife the Cloaths on her Back.

We must take them as we find
them, our new lovers are all
as mannered as a maitre d'

in presenting themselves,
ensconced in the garnish
of histories, hazy bios

in recesses beyond our common
era, wonderful, heathen lives,
and if we had known them then,

in those ancient times, we might
have laughed at them, they at us
and our clothes (I needn't recall

those old styles here, serious
black, drugged paisley, or worse),
and we might have returned them

and their young, stylized poses,
to their imperfect first loves,
those who were chipping away

at their youth, grinding down
their jagged fantasies so later
we could find ourselves within

their storied arms at last,
their clothing borrowed, stolen
and God knows saved until

they become the very selves
we have discovered, finally
here, rumpled but good as new.

OF PHILOSOPHY

THE PHENOMENOLOGY OF WINTER

The Force of Nature is the Greatest

When the dark solstice closes
the doors, slams the shutters
and unravels the shades as

it eases out the light,
trims day at both ends,
then I imagine one beam

stretching longer, thinner,
a holy reach which cannot
dispel the arctic camp

such cooling pitches.
It is only a day ending,
despite descriptions like

> *The Blizzard of the Century*
> *or the Fifty Year Snow-Event*

which happens every other year,
the fatalistic snow drifts
which we might predict
in horoscopes:

> *Your day will be stopped*
> *before it begins. Do not*
> *let the inevitable falling*
> *crush, chill or trap you.*

Light flees
at four p.m.
(I can see nothing so
nothing is) and then
I cannot locate
the stars as the tent
flap of clouds has closed
for the night. The radio
issues a prospectus
on the fine-as-dust income
of a storm day, never falling
hard but falling still,

like the failing light
as sure as plumb lines.
The forecast proclaims
a *nor'easter* which means:

It's coming. You're next.

Hill Country Hegemony

The Law favoreth some Persons:
married Women, Infants, Ideots
and Mad-men.

Life on hungry hills
in the Appalachian mountains,
was favored over all fruits
of the valleys—there we'd hide
our base, idiot selves,
rave with our mad-limbs,
tame raccoons to perch
on our shoulders and when given
watches not care if we cannot
decipher the diachronic faces,
believing instead in potions,
amulets and signs, pouches
of bone, hair and soil for seizures,
split black beans buried by midnight,
for love or to relieve other pains.

But the sheer rise of earth
was a divine nudge, the whole
mass of words we knew
from the Bible, lovely,
wise and unknowable,
was ours, by God, ours.
The spring brought us laurel,
white tufts of truth,

a mayflower to protect us,
and jack-in-the-pulpits

to offer feral sermons
beneath the ferns
and hemlock stands.
Through them, courses
of bears trample springs
doused by gravity,
and we bend to them
for a free sip of ice
water married with crystal.

That's all part of why we came,
following markings, tramroads,
enduring the taunt of bedrock
and clay. We could laugh at
the world. There are even times
when the sun stupidly impales itself
on the mountains on the way down.

Materialism or All of the Good Jazz Vocalists Are Dead

A Man's Person before his Possession.

Well, at least it's new, my family
will say, as though that's a proof
of value, and what we cannot replace
we paint so *at least it's clean.*

We eschew the junkshop.
If it's on sale, everything's
a bargain at the Mart. New
usurps the past, the recent
surpasses itself.

First we lived in mountain
houses, then the transition
of trailers, a passage through
rent to own—finally we had
a shiny place, with the best
appliances, an ivory plain
of drywall, formica and new
cars with black chin guards,
old gleaming chrome bumpers,
Dali moustaches across front
and rear, streamlined body
without wings, gone.

The new gaudily climbs
our bodies like boas,
onto our cupboards as latex oak,
or between us like plexi-glass.

I am cursed by a confidence game
of plastic, the chaos of waferboard,
an incest of fingerlath, a fatalism
of vinyl and the perjury of veneer.

I want the groan of plank under
my feet, a stony slap of plaster,
the genuine plying of lips
when I love, only Billie Holiday
on the radio, every night, singing:

*I go to bed with the prayer
that you'll make love to me,
strange as it seems.*

I want that sweet old used to be,
I will not settle for the drum
machine of the new—you can have it
—the efficient present tense.

VICARIOUS

A Villain set free for an hour will
be always free.

I am fumbling in the newspapers
and read of a post office turned
free-fire zone, and I think

about the word *disgruntled*
evoking as much indigestion
as rage. I am afraid some

switch has been flipped,
and villains who once sneered
and twirled tell-tale mustaches,

now look as blank as Bauhaus walls
and flinch only in a recoil
of weapons. I fold and refold

the paper, watch as a young man
shunks quarters into a machine.
I see him bending to his work,

intent upon his digital mayhem,
and catch glimmers of fires
in the faces of Visigoths,

the glint of a thatch of arrows
filling the air of a city beset
by the Khan's horde, and I see

in his hunched back, frantic hands
holding the machine like it would
run away from him, that we will

never be settled, never be able
to live with the dying we cause in
our free hours, in our spare time.

OF POLITICAL
AND MORAL RULES

Junkshop Reprise

*The Law favoreth a Thing that
is of Necessity.*

They are spawned everywhere
necessary, the shops of flim
and the curb-borne, dregs

of the cellar, attic and shed,
the discounted and debilitated,
as needed as bacteria releasing

the fallen into living loam.
These farouche collectors
bear the nubilous spread

of our waste, they signify us
with outlaw storefronts and
in webby bosoms of barns,

and with a casual strength
gleaned from gathering, hauling
and imagining all of the prices

we must reject in the haggle,
the deal, the give-it-to-me-for,
as we acquire the revenant

props, stashed and saved nuances
lending irony to our owning
the property of the long gone,

robbed from the daily caravans
of dumptrucks, the fragile cargo
of the carnage from the new taking

umbrage with the old, the undone,
the unusual and the usable still,
the bartered and the battered,

eschewed then found and fondled
in our new hands, these blossoms,
sweet baubles, good bounty,

until we are sold and carry it
to the man at the glass counter
full of odds-and-ends, gewgaws,

flamfleur, bric-a-brac, stuff
like watches, medals, inkpens
grinning figures from an ancient

World's Fair, and even pocketknives
fresh from the remembered hands
of our grandfathers. We ask

What is the price, knowing full
damn well the value, the anonymity
we hope to shed in owning a book

we know was written so long ago
only we would crack its pages
to find and salvage the words.

BASIC NECESSITIES

Necessity is of three Sorts.

1. *Necessity of Conservation of Life*

Runners beat their own
time, their best start,
and can recite the proteins,
fibers and loathsome fats

of the last snack or rare
full meal, but others
keep declaring the last
drink, the final smoke,

vowing this time it's over.

Water and mud grapple our legs
as we raise M-1 rifles above
our heads, in the paddies of life-
giving rice, the burning place

we must search and purge,
our buddies at our elbows,
but when one shatters over
a mine, at first we are

as glad as Ivan Ilych's friends.

Infants will pull their heads
out of water or stop
when coaxed to crawl over

a sheet of plexi-glass

their mothers calling them,
but when grown we will stand
on a cliff, feathering our hearts
with maybe, legs aching

for the clear jump out.

2. *Necessity of Obedience*

The law.
We are made
to beat ourselves
for the sake
of ourselves.

Spare me
your Norman Vincent Peale
rant about the uplifting,
eighty-six your desire
for wonder or fuzzy
epiphanies in metaphors
which repeat and rise.
I'm chanting my way
out of this:

Bow to the god of love
and then find betrayal.
Tithe to the lord of art
and then endure censor.
Follow the law of nature
and then weather tornado.

Honor the act of virtue
and embrace the cutthroat.
Entreat the muse of war
and lose first necessity.
It is this simple:

Trust and pray, hope
and obey
and then

beat yourself
for the sake
of yourself.

That's what it gets you.

3. *Necessity of the Act of God*

A man, full and hearty,
drops dead at the bowling alley,
at once as still and breathless,
as the parquet floor beneath him,
and someone will pipe up
that he was spied ordering
salt bagels at the deli,
with God-knows-what on them.

The limb comes down,
the big one from the silver maple
as old as the house, and
a neighbor will say the tree
was a menace and should have
been cut down before it ruined

the porch. Go out in a crush
of metal and speed and your loose
seatbelt will hang incriminations.

Embrace the fickle life
of another and at least
blame time for the later
estrangement. Spend your days
looking into the twisting mirror
of self, and that will be
dismissed as a consumption,
absorption, a self-prayer.

But witness
this act of conservation,
this poem for prayer, this plea
for art and life and for the oldest
tree, unbroken, unbeholden still.
A witness is necessary in all things,
even if we use gods for audiences,
obediently clapping their creative hands
at all the right places (how could they
be wrong), at all the best lines.

TAKING MEALS

First of Conservation of Life, if a Man
steal Viands to satisfy his present
Hunger, this is not Felony or Larceny.

In the spring we drift
down to Saint E's Hospital
to eat in the sunbright
cafeteria, the cheapest
meal next to St. Vincent's
shelter, and then we return
to our shadow of a house,
the beat oak woodwork,
the curtainless windows,
the kitchen and its bounty
of garbage and soiled dishes,
where we hide from each
other, as our sight keys
a hymn of hunger. Sometimes
Mateo can slip inside
a grocery, and in a zipped
marsupial Eisenhower jacket,
retrieve cartons of smokes,
or when we are quite beside
ourselves, a ready-made sub
which we share like crows.
In the summer I work
three jobs, nightshift cleaning
libraries, grinding old scales
of floor wax for a coke-head
boss who never pays until we
chase him down, where we watch

archival movies in the backroom
and eat armloads of books.
Afternoon shift is a truckstop,
washing dishes, clearing tables,
weighing haddock slabs or
spinning the skins off spuds,
and then I spend the day
painting and papering an empty
apartment where I sleep on
two sofa cushions, and earn
rights to stay another night,
to another breakfast at Custard's
Last Stand across the street,
a late lunch between dishloads,
dinner however I can get it.

THE SAPPER

So if a Fire be in a Street, I may
justify the pulling down of the Wall
or House of another Man to save the
Row from the spreading of the Fire.

A sapper is a sly punch,
like the one I saw given

      to a drunken challenge,
      a swerving, stormy body

who reminded me of my father
when he angered himself with liquor.

      But this man before me
      was caught between gravity
      and confused muscles.
      I had backed into his car,
      and when he saw it, all
      was fire and threat, inner
      borealis. He bellowed
      like a baseball manager
      and I waited on a moment,

my old denim jacket
half-slipped off, almost
ready—then the man

      buckled like he had
      been yanked to the earth
      by a leash.

Behind my back, Snork scolded me
for binding my fists in sleeves.
He had reached over my shoulder
and put the man down with a blow.

And sometime, to sap the flames,
I'd pour out a bit of whiskey,
adding water to quell

the rage, keeping the bottle
full for the man who knows what
I did might have been necessary
to save the burning house.

CELL DIVISION

The Husband and Wife are one Person.

It is the measured partition
of the petals of a blossom,
prying fingers apart
so they forget the others
in work or prayer.

It was Aristophanes, not Aristotle,
who reasoned this one out,
but he was wrong: There is no
half-self looking for another
to make *the beast with two backs.*
Let's get one thing straight,
only in division does unity
matter. Joined in sheets,
cups, pictures, music, chairs,
books, wills and desires,

—all must be severed.
How do you say *I'll take Kafka,
you take Tolstoy* as though
passing great thoughts across
a canyon, staking out
new wildernesses. Bodies
are always separate,

never truly linked,
remaining vessels waiting
for what the heart needs,
though each chamber
empties as the other fills.

STEEL MILL DOMESTIC

*A Husband hath power over his
Wife's Person; but if he threaten
to kill her &c., She may make him
security for the Peace.*

How do you bear the amorphous
brooding? Even the bluest
eye winks darkly in the factory,
the air a filtering black,

the noise a slap to the ear,
so he must fight the bastards
for a sound barrier and declare
the world is less distinct,

but at night it is the weight
of work which hunkers him,
as he brings home the blast
furnace and its hot spume.

Then it gets too dark for mirrors
for either man or woman, night
cools and hardens between them,
and he is brought to spew out

and you must listen hard to hear
as he breaks up under his loud
and filthy day, and you must counter
his coughing by calmly breathing.

WHAT I HAVE NO NEED TO LEARN

The Law compelleth no One to
Impossibilities

Someone wants a high shelf,
but there is nothing
to fashion it to, no wall,

so we invent skyhooks, claim
they will hold it all like Atlas.

Archimedes claimed he could,
with a long enough lever
and a place to stand,
move the world, but I am

glad we are not asked to fly,
as I can imagine how
that would complicate
adolescence, forced

to embrace that leap as well.
I am thankful not to

coax the lilac out onto tips
of winter-brittled branches,
pull newborns out of suckling

clay or make my bed as I lie
in it. We are not compelled

to wake in a swirling nautilus,
and crawling out, evolve
ourselves each morning,

or maintain any corruptible
form but the feeble trappings
lent us. And if the pulse

races, twirls or stomps,
it is keeping its own beastly
time as the body is a train
on temporal tracks while we are
free to meander and be lost.

AGENCY

He who acts by Another is held to act by
Himself

1. "Ouija Board Sweeps Town"

From the March 5, 1920,
New York *Evening Sun*:

In El Cerrito, California,
a mass meeting in the town hall
last night decided that every
one of the 1,200 citizens should
be examined by mental experts
to determine if the ouija board
craze has got them.

The El Cerrito citizen's decision
followed the arrest of seven persons
there on charges of insanity after
they had become ouija board fiends.

A friend declares the ouija
is the perfect toy:
It does nothing, and you can
only play with it if someone
cheats. But I remember
sitting in the cellar,
as stone-gloomy a place as
we had, with its forbidden
coal bin, penumbral corners,
and my sister and I queried

the board. A spirit, the other,
skittered the tiny table under
our fingertips, to *yes* and *no*,
to words one letter at a time.

We both swore we never pushed
the pointer, that it really
possessed us, children
thrilled, children worried
that their lives would remain
such powerful and small
mediums for tomorrow.
I know I never pushed it.

2. "Mass Graves Found"

I am quite culpable for acts
which have thrust themselves
upon me: wasted kisses,
curses given and received,
secret messages—it should be
easy to know who is to blame.

Some days the guilty can
duck, bob and weave,
doing the rope-a-dope
of truth, so it is

in the Balkans where
it is hard to tell who
had to die. Here I must
transmit the mournful,
so stay with me, keep
your hands on the table.

I see
them standing at a trench
waiting for the blossoms
of their backs and skulls.
They want you to know.
Look closely

at your hands, could they
direct the weapon? Someone
is guiding this thing,
I promise you, it cannot
be happening, cannot be

telling me this.
Impossible. Let me go,
get your breath out
of my ear. Someone,
please turn on the light.

OF TENURES, DEEDS & HEIR

SANCTUARY

A Man hath but two Ages: The full Age
of Male and Female is one and twenty.

Twelve college men march
through the women's dormitory,
twelve college men with penises
and pockets out, what they call

The Elephant Walk. But they
are couched in metaphor,
protected like loons yodeling
over north country lakes.

In schools well-greened
and bricked, tuition stands
as bail against such foul play,
where they form pacts, howl

well. But I live next door
to Carl, nineteen and broke,
sometimes working, mostly not,
often in bars, who shows up

at my door, wrist shattered
in a brawl. He has a habitat
of needs: money for rent,
food, gas, smokes, and things

less or more solid, like a gift
of love poetry for a woman
which I actually give to him,
a cheap volume of Dickinson.

He chugs along, full, brawny,
with an impossible future,
once telling me he'd go back
to school if he could find

how to survive there, but one
dank mood, one unrestorable night,
he is captured, soaring drunk
and pounding holes in the walls

of his apartment. He is evicted
from the barren shell, barred
from what he has, no shield, all
very real, with no one to disrupt

but himself. I watch him wander
for a day, imploring, even weeping,
then he disappears, extinct or
simply graduated to another place.

THE RITES

A Woman hath six Ages; The Lord her
Father may distrain for Aid for her Marriage
when She is seven. She is double at nine.
She is able to assent to Matrimony at
twelve.She shall not be inward if she be
fourteen. She shall go out of Ward at sixteen.
She may sell or give her Lands at one and
twenty.

Some women assume hazard
with every age. A woman
endures her father's rages,
geared to drink and agonies,
as he tears up the new
wallpaper with a knife.

He is double the trouble
when she is nine, a horror
at twelve when she meets
the man she would love
by fourteen, need by sixteen.

Her father is dead one morning
by her twentieth birthday.
But nothing ends here,
with more ages to weather,
bad fronts moving in.
By thirty, her man takes
to drink after a factory
day, and then becomes
his own foment. He wanders,

but she keeps this rank,
black lily alive until light
comes in with middle age,
when he sees his own contour
as bestial and he stops

the drink, danger clearing
like a humid haze.
But she has so submerged
herself in the anger of men
she has grown not stronger,
but coarser, a residue
of salt, an unflinching
pillar at his side.

FOR AMELIA EARHART

Conveyance of a Woman covert is void.

You might find her if you looked:

curled up in a chest
in the back of a north
bound wagon, or dead
drunk and lucky, stuffed
in a whiskey barrel and
thrown over Niagara Falls
—a true story. She was
the one and nearly only
person to survive the stunt,
though many tried, men
in exquisite capsules,
until the fool enterprise
was outlawed. She is hidden

everywhere, in the stars,
in her Amherst bedroom,
donning a bugler's gear,
a deck-hand's cap, or goggles
and leathers, flying across
the Pacific, leaving behind
a shoe and a signal—flying

right into the void, the hiding
place of history. The sea flapped
back to receive her as it might
once have Odysseus, the waves
punting her fuselage like a barrel.

We look for her, our most strayed
lover, radio broadcasts
of the loss recited on the hour.

JUNK MIRROR

And if any Writing be read in any other
Form to a Man unlearned, It shall not be
His
although he seal and deliver it.

My broken, black-and-white
television sits on the radio
in the living room. It once
worked, but when the picture
narrowed and zipped away,

I left it sitting there,
artifact of the aliterate.

Did you see that on TV?
I am asked, and I nod,
though the machine's black
eye is my only such sight,
my only memory of television
is antique: Gleason moon,
Lucy heart. Am I a living

witness to a golden age?
That's what the neo-oral
crowd says, as surely as
they know the nightly

spatter of sitcoms, the longer
rise and fall of police shows,
the enforced, two-hour regularity
of movies, made-for or adapted.

And the news, the now, goes on,

the head saying,
Today she died, tomorrow
they meet, and weather
is here while the ten-inch
screen in my room shows only
me in its convex reflection.

Last Go-Round

If any Man offer to take away My Goods I
may lay My Hands upon Him, and rather
beat Him than suffer Him to carry Them
away.

It might be in a rhomboid barn,
the door slid at a caterwonk,
full of our material nepenthe.
I saw an old bed frame filled

with a trough where the springs
once heaved with love and dreams,
now sprouting brash marigolds.
A flower bed its junkman owner

said through a scratched grin.
There are new uses for everything,
and no one's around to stop us.
We are the worst of thieves.

There are planks astraddle cement
blocks in a front yard, covered
in tools, and we can buy them
all, the files and clamps and

bolt cutters, or the rows of book
spines showing the inner workings
like fossils in matrix—these
we can choose and store and maybe

read when they emerge again.
And the junkshop can have secrets:
lover's names in dedicated volumes,
a new way to refasten an axe handle,

or the trunk, box, chest full
of *dearest* notes, linens, locks
and godly books with the births
of the dead clearly marked, or even

a little case with drawers full
of knives and honing stones,
blades as sharp as good questions,
and other small items we cannot

understand. In the junkshop I
can even find myself, tucked away
on a shelf like a worn appliance
waiting to be fixed and claimed.

TWILIGHT TRESPASS

No Law or Statute doth charge the
Heir for the Wrong or Trespass of
His Father, but by express Words.

All this long year,
I have jolted from sleep
every two hours, regular
as a work-day, seized
by *Something is wrong,*

and it takes me minutes
to decide if it is true,
the pipes tinking steam
in the winter, a fan
chanting in the summer.
And something *is* wrong,
but I eventually nod
to the next intersection.

To find sleep, I imagine,
travelling down roads.
It might be a two-lane
south of Marietta, Ohio,
or one of the canopied lanes
through rich suburbs north
of Youngstown, but lately

I've found myself on
a scoured road through
sage, a seared New Mexico
slipping in my peripheral

—no relief in that sight,
sins spread out behind
and before me, the sameness,
stillness, is wrong, all wrong.

* * *

General Pickett's charge
in Gettysburg was fraught
with error, twelve thousand
soldiers parade ground marching
over five hundred open yards,
exposed to an army of enemies,
like walking into a wild wind.

Today that field is hayed,
or made up in corn or wheat
on the old Eisenhower farm,
that general having retired
to a failing heart. Meade
and Lee stand at the ends
in the polished stasis
of angels, in New Hampshire
granite, Virginia limestone.

I have walked over that ground,
have dodged and *fear'd*, the field
strewn with lead and buttons,
bones born over in spring thaw.
The sins of the fathers also rise
in burdock, flox and thistle along
the path. If I wake tonight,

I'll try walking that route,
not a road but a direction,
where salvation is behind,
dumb bravery ahead—there I
will not be weighed by a next
hour or day, what is wrong will
be as obvious as the dawn.

* * *

This evening, seven young men,
as old as they'd need to be
to die in Gettysburg,
slip and shimmy on skateboards,
tacking against the curbs
and barriers of the sullen
county parking lot. They move
like saints in the hum of grace,
like dreamers, arms pinwheeling

in balance and joy. What I do
not want to notice are those
moments when they grow tired,
when they sit on the retaining
wall, or walk home, clothes
flapping over their bodies.
Then they stare at their feet,
as though suddenly finding them
at the end of such long legs,
wondering how they know to

keep marching home, or in mistaken
directions where they might love,

but where they later will surely
sleep, hearty and full, dreaming
what I do not want to remember,
wishing they need not awaken
to wrongs they finally must know.

The Final Deliberations

*I will here conclude, requesting all those to
whom My Sight, hereof shall or   may
happen to come, friendly to admonish Me of
My Failings herein, whereby They shall
engage Me then fully.*

I have broken all of these laws,
I confess, and I love Aristotle
for his certainty, Dee for magic,
Amelia for her impossibility
—all of them for bearing me,
this much should be clear.

But there are no laws,
do not look for guidance
here, irreducible maxims
or firm ground. I have sown

mutations, intended to veer
from the long ago plotted path,
like a train scissor-backing
an Allegheny mountain side.
This is a handbook of errors,
missed steps, the railing gone,
unleashed arms flailing like gyres.

Something broken is junk,
so I salvage what I can,
looking through the warped lens
of memory, seeking poetic justice.
This is a disclaimer for all

we believe about the insensible
world. If you look there you

will find me, eating my meals,
forgiving my father, forgiving
your father too. I'll be waiting
my turn, always polite, and I'll
be that thin man you barely see,
bent triple under the bargain table,
looking at the books still in boxes,
the ones they do not even hope
to sell. I'll stand up suddenly,
volume in hand, and walk away,
head gone batty with memories
and the promise of words. I'll be
the guy you swore saved you,
hailed you, loved you—yes
him too. When you see me
stop and set me straight,
tell me not to mourn the fallen,
lost or divine, the last hand
on the creased page, on my own.
But first,

accept this much, take it
like a photograph, and then
make up your own myths, please
do, the necessary ones, so we
will have something to embrace,
something when you and I need
a few rules to find our way.

Naton Leslie's poems have appeared in *The Massachusetts Review*, *The Ohio Review*, *Puerto Del Sol*, *Prairie Schooner*, *The Chariton Review* and other literary journals. A recipient of a fellowship in poetry from the National Endowment for the Arts, his previous books are *Moving to Find Work* (Bottom Dog Press, 2000) and *Their Shadows Are Dark Daughters* (Pavement Saw Press, 1998). He lives in Saratoga Springs, New York and is associate professor of English at Siena College in Loudonville, New York.

MAY   2011

9 780970 866677